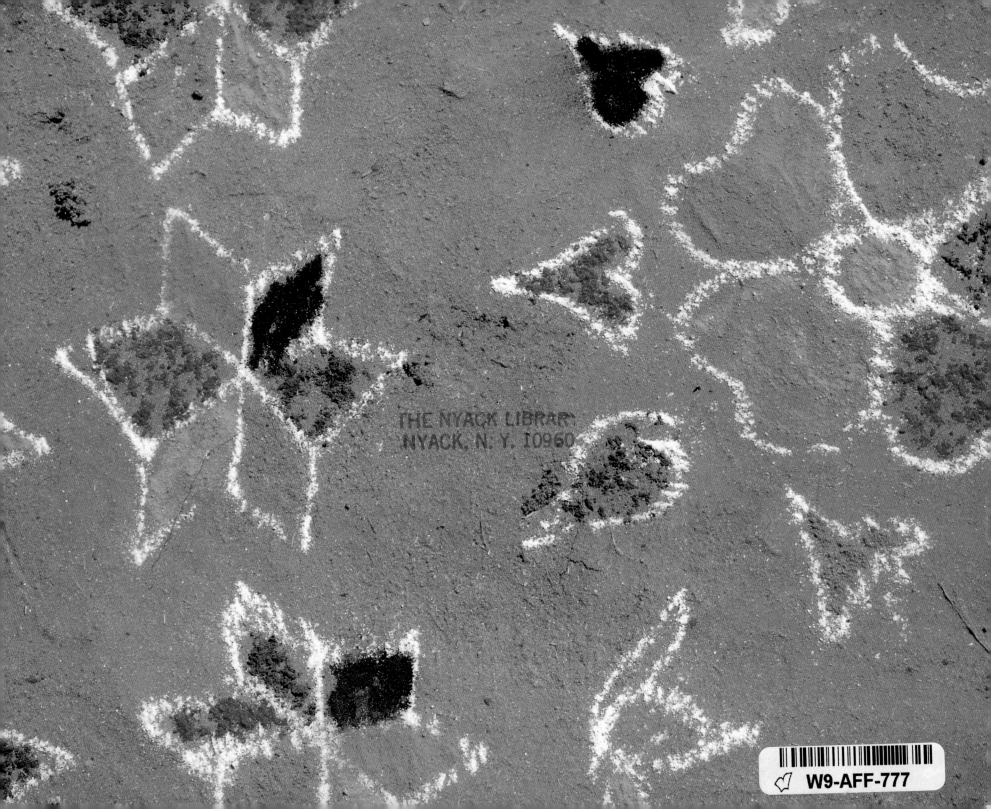

To Amrita, Prita, Shaun and Shauna for inspiring me,
and to Yvonne for support and advice

I is for India copyright © Frances Lincoln Limited 1996
Text and photographs copyright © Prodeepta Das 1996
The Publishers would like to acknowledge Ifeoma Onyefulu as the originator of the series
of which this book forms a part. Ifeoma Onyefulu is the author and photographer of *A is for Africa*.

First published in Great Britain in 1996 by Frances Lincoln Limited,
4 Torriano Mews, Torriano Avenue, London NW5 2RZ

Published in the United States in 1997 by
Silver Press
A Division of Simon & Schuster
299 Jefferson Road
Parsippany, NJ 07054-0408

Printed in Hong Kong

10 9 8 7 6 5 4 3 2 1

Library of Congress Cataloging-in-Publication Data
Das, Prodeepta.
I is for India/by Prodeepta Das.
Summary: An alphabetical listing of historical and cultural information on India.
ISBN 0-382-39278-7 (LSB) ISBN 0-382-39279-5 (PBK)
1. India-Juvenile literature. [1. India.] 1. Title
DS407.D35 1997   95-43424
954-dc20   CIP
                                AC

I is for INDIA

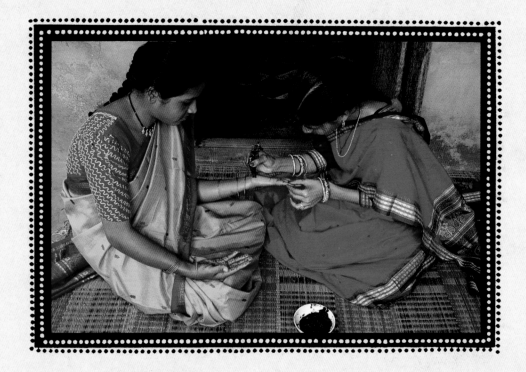

Prodeepta Das

Silver Press

AUTHOR'S NOTE

India is a continent with a long, rich history, now venturing bravely toward the twenty-first century.

It is full of surprising contrasts: vast open landscapes and small towns bursting at the seams; Hindus, Moslems, Sikhs, Christians and many other religions, often existing side by side, each with its own form of worship and way of life; quiet villages and sprawling cities where social changes take place at a dizzying rate. Nevertheless, some things are the same everywhere: the warmth of the people, their zest for life, and their fondness for rich colors.

I come from Orissa, in eastern India, and the words and images in this book reflect the India that I know and love. I hope they will inspire young people to go further and explore the color, excitement and mystery of this great continent.

Prodeepta

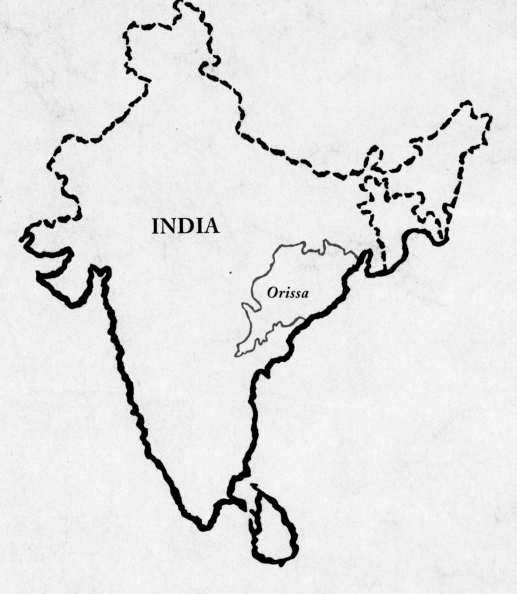

INDIA

Orissa

Aa is for the Alphabet children learn at school. India has many languages, each with its own alphabet. These village schoolchildren are learning Oriya, the alphabet of the state of Orissa. Their teacher writes out the first few letters on each child's slate, and then the children call out the letters as they go over them.

is for Bullock cart, used for carrying people and goods along the city streets and the dusty roads of the countryside. The cart has two big wooden wheels and is pulled by one or two bullocks, or young bulls. As roads are improved and people are traveling by bus, car and motorcycle, bullock carts are being used mostly for transporting goods.

is for Cinema, or movie theater. Most people living outside the cities have no television, so going to the movies is a favorite way for families to spend their spare time. Huge billboards advertise the movies that are playing locally, and people stand in line for hours to see their favorite stars. Indian films are packed with song and dance.

D d is for Diwali, the Festival of Lights. It is a celebration of the Hindu god Rama's return home after 12 years in exile in the jungle. Everywhere, houses glow from lighted earthenware lamps placed on verandas, rooftops, walls, and windowsills. Children wear new clothes for the festival, and families gather to set off fireworks.

Ee

is for Elephant, an animal feared by all other jungle creatures. Elephants in India have smaller ears and teeth than elephants in Africa. Tamed elephants have always been used to carry people and heavy goods. Now, as the forests disappear and people are using trucks more and more, national parks and forest provide elephants with safe places to live.

F f is for Family and Family life, which is very strong in India. In the villages, members of several generations live under the same roof, but in crowded cities this is not always possible. Children learn when very young to respect their elders, who have special places in the families.

G g

is for Gold, which
people love to buy and
wear. When an Indian girl
is small, she has her ears
pierced and wears gold
studs. Later, when she
marries, she is given gold
and silver jewelery by her
relatives, and she wears
much of it for her wedding.

Hh

is for Haat or markets, which are held in the open air and some in covered stalls. People come from all around to buy and sell fruit, vegetables, grain, spices, clothes and many other things. Haat are cheap, colourful and extremely noisy places!

I i

is for India, a vast country with a population of many millions. India's people speak 17 different languages, follow many different religions, and live in every kind of landscape—from hot deserts and plains to cold mountainous areas—but everyone is warm and friendly and proud to be Indian.

J j is for Jilabi, a mouthwatering, crunchy yellow sweet. To make it, the sweet-maker presses chickpea-flour batter through a mold into a deep pan of boiling oil to fry, until it looks like a fat spider's web. Then after a dipping in sugar syrup, it is ready to eat.

K k

K k is for Kameez, a loose tunic that women and girls all over India like to wear. The tunics are made in many different styles and in every color imaginable. Some are hand-woven and decorated with beautiful embroidery.

is for Lassi, a refreshing yogurt drink made from cow's or goat's milk. Seasoned with salt and pepper, it is cooling and soothing, but it tastes equally delicious sweetened with nuts and spices.

is for Mehndi, a tattoolike decoration often worn by young women at weddings and festivals. The beautician grinds henna leaves with oil, making a green paste. Then she squeezes the paste through a cone to make patterns on the customer's hands and feet. As a design dries, it turns bright red. It can be washed off later with water.

is for Namaskar or Namaste—hands folded and held up in greeting. It is our way of saying, "I respect you."

is for Odissi, an ancient traditional dance. In the past, the odissi was only performed in temples by men and women wearing special silk saris, crowns, and ankle bells. Now it can take place anywhere. It is one of the four most important Indian classical dances and, like ballet, takes many years of training to perform it well.

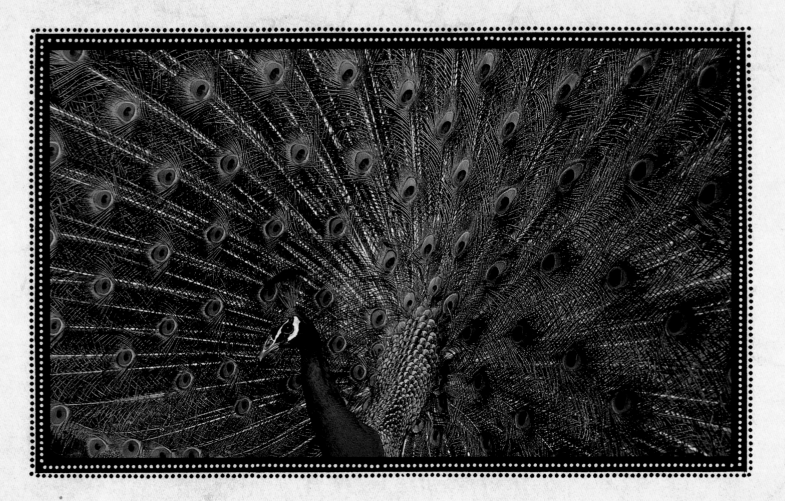

is for Peacock, India's national bird. People believe that peacocks come out to dance when it is going to rain. The birds spread out their beautiful plumes like a fan when they are courting, just before the monsoon season begins.

Qq

is for the Quran or Koran, the book of the prophet Mohammed which Muslim children learn from when they are very young. They sit on prayer mats facing in the direction of the holy city of Mecca and read aloud from the pages of the Quran, which is printed in beautiful Arabic letters.

R r is for Rice, which is eaten boiled, fried or made into cakes or puddings. The rice is planted when the rains come. Once the young green plants have turned into rich golden brown, families work together cutting, threshing, and winnowing the grain. Rice is everywhere: it is used during religious ceremonies, at weddings; colored rice powder even decorates the walls and floors.

Ss

is for Sadhu or holy man.
You can tell a sadhu by his long
hair and beard, by the special
marks on his forehead, by his
necklace and his loincloth.
Sadhus have chosen to leave their
families and possessions to spend
all their time praying. People
respect their way of life and give
them food and drink. Some
sadhus stay in one place, but
others travel around, sleeping in
temples or outside—wherever
they happen to be.

T t is for Tea, growing on the high slopes of eastern and southern India. Tea pickers gather only the top two leaves and a bud from the tips of each bush. Once the green tea leaves have been crushed and dried, they become a deep brown. At the tea stalls, tea or *chay,* made with water, milk, and sugar, is kept brewing and is served in small glasses. Some people like to add the spices cardamom and ginger to make masala tea.

Uu is for Umbrella, used not only when it rains but also to give shade from the hot sun. The most beautiful umbrellas are made in the small village of Pipili in the state of Orissa.

Vv is for Veena, an ancient Indian musical instrument with seven strings. It is made from a piece of jackfruit wood, with a hollow at the top end. The veena takes many years to learn to play.

is for Water. In the rainy season there is too much of it, and in the dry season too little. Many towns only receive piped water for a few hours each day, so everyone stores it in big containers to have enough for the rest of the day. In the villages, people collect rain water in tanks or sink deep wells. People use the rivers, canals and ponds for washing, watering crops, and keeping cattle clean. Ritual bathing is done in the holy river at Varanasi and in the sea at Puri.

is for Xmas, as Christmas is usually known in India. It is a time when Christian families gather together to receive presents from Father Xmas and to pose solemnly for a great family photograph. In southern India, Xmas is celebrated in January.

Yy is for Yatra, a religious fair often held in a temple. Pilgrims, holy men, and people of all ages come from near and far to worship, listen to songs of prayer, and watch shows based on stories from holy books. Sometimes, when a yatra goes on for a few days, people sleep outside in tents.

is for the Zodiac, or *Greha*, of 12 birth signs in astrology. The zodiac is very important to the Indian people, whatever their religion. It is based on a 3,000 year old Sanskrit manuscript. When a baby is born, an astrologer, or *joytish*, is called in to work out the baby's birth sign. He makes calculations in chalk on the floor and writes them on a palm leaf with an iron pen. The leaf is then wrapped in a clean cloth and treasured by the parents together with their own hopes for the baby's future.

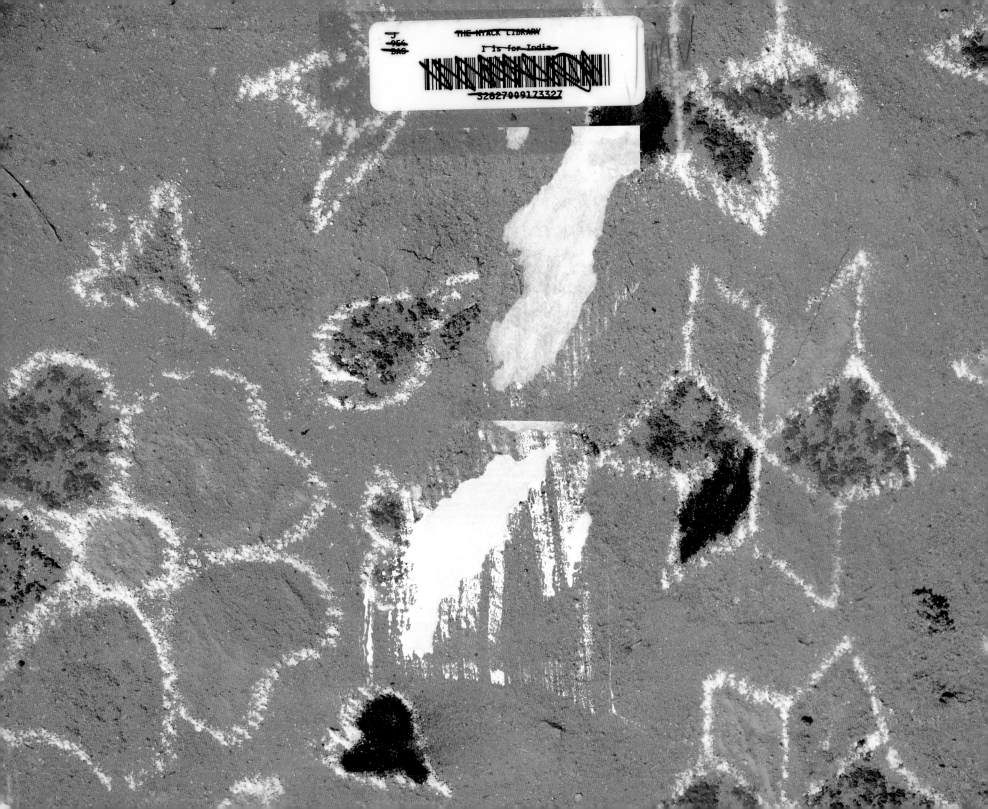